12 Days of Christmas

Scripture quotations are from the New Revised Standard Version of the Bible,
Anglicized Edition, copyright © 1989, 1995 by the Division of Christian Education of
the National Council of the Churches in Christ in the USA. Used by permission. All
rights reserved.

Printed in the UK by Core Publications Limited, Kettering

AN INVITATION TO ... FOLLOW THE STAR

by Archbishop Stephen Cottrell

If there's one thing just about everyone knows about the Christmas story, it's that the Wise Men followed a star, and that the star signified the birth of a new king.

And because we know the story so well, we don't examine it much. We think we know what it means. But as we begin another Christmas, I think it's important to focus on one of the more neglected aspects of the story: the moment when the Wise Men stop following the star. They follow it for many miles to begin with, but when their destination gets near they choose to follow their own wisdom instead. They put their trust in their own charts and their own understanding. Instead of following the star, they visit King Herod.

After all, isn't a palace where a new-born king is most likely to be found?

Read **Matthew 2.1-6**

In the time of King Herod, after Jesus was born in Bethlehem of Judea, wise men from the East came to Jerusalem, asking, 'Where is the child who has been born king of the Jews? For we observed his star at its rising, and have come to pay him homage...' Calling together all the chief priests and scribes of the people, Herod inquired of them where the Messiah was to be born. They told him, 'In Bethlehem of Judea; for so it has been written by the prophet ...'

Reflection

Exactly how wise are these Wise Men? And whose wisdom do we follow? These are some of the questions this story raises.

Arriving at Herod's palace to see the new king and pay him homage, the Wise Men are not only in the wrong place, they're jeopardising the very thing they've come to honour. Herod, fearful for his own position, calls his scribes together. Consulting the ancient wisdom of the words of Scripture, they direct the Wise Men towards Bethlehem.

Following Jesus isn't easy. Other bright lights entice and fascinate. We can end up preferring our own ideas and trusting our own wisdom. We can finish up in the wrong place doing the wrong things. Only the light of Jesus – God's Living Word – endures. And it leads to unexpected places: to God found in stables, not palaces.

INVITATION

The invitation to all of us this Christmas Eve is to be re-directed towards the light that is Christ, and to allow ourselves to be surprised and delighted by where it leads us.

Jesus, Light of the World, be a light to our feet, and a lantern on our path, this Christmas Eve and always. Amen.

AN INVITATION TO ... SHARE GOOD NEWS

by Naomi Metzger

When I was young I really had no idea I would become an athlete.

I didn't play many sports as a child. I had poor hand–eye coordination and I dreamed of pursuing other things. However, I gradually came to feel God wanted me to do sports for a bigger purpose.

But when training felt hard and competitions went badly, I started to question if this was my purpose and wondered what God wanted me to do with my talent.

Then a few months ago, I got a message from a supporter. He said that watching me compete and the small interactions we had really helped him when he was in a really dark period of his life. It then dawned on me that one of my purposes for being an athlete wasn't the medals or the titles – but spreading joy.

The angel said to the shepherds, 'Do not be afraid; for see—I am bringing you good news of great joy for all the people: to you is born this day in the city of David a Saviour, who is the Messiah, the Lord …' When the angels had left them and gone into heaven, the shepherds said to one another, 'Let us go now to Bethlehem and see this thing that has taken place, which the Lord has made known to us.' So they went with haste and found Mary and Joseph, and the child lying in the manger.

Reflection

The shepherds were the last people you'd expect to hear the good news directly from the angels. They were just ordinary folk doing their unglamorous work. When they became shepherds, they would have thought their main purpose was to look after sheep and that was all. However, once they had received this news, they became a staple part in the biggest story ever and they helped to spread the good news to everyone. Sometimes we can all feel ordinary or that we can't have much impact. But our seemingly small actions – such as checking up on a friend, helping a stranger in the shops or even just smiling at someone – can have a profound and lasting effect of spreading joy to the world around us. Today, like the shepherds, let's make haste to find simple, ordinary ways to share the extraordinary joy of Christmas with others.

INVITATION

Wherever you are today – with others or on your own –
look for simple, ordinary ways you can spread a little
of the extraordinary joy of Christmas.

Lord, thank you for all you have given us. Help us to share our gifts, our joy and our love with the world around us. Amen.

AN INVITATION TO … COME AND SEE

by Victoria Johnson

Of all the words spoken during our services to mark Christmas each year, perhaps the most profound come from the start of St John's Gospel: 'And the Word was made flesh and dwelt among us'. Today the Church celebrates the feast of St John and the many powerful words he contributed to the New Testament.

But, if we flick forward to the very end of his Gospel, John admits all the books in the world cannot contain everything one would wish to say about Jesus. Powerful as they can be, John says, words are never quite enough.

Words need to lead to life, just as the Word became flesh and lived among us. What we read – and what we say we believe – needs to be translated into a way of living.

Read John 1.35-41

The next day John again was standing with two of his disciples, and as he watched Jesus walk by, he exclaimed, 'Look, here is the Lamb of God!' The two disciples heard him say this, and they followed Jesus. When Jesus turned and saw them following, he said to them, 'What are you looking for?' They said to him, 'Rabbi' (which translated means Teacher), 'where are you staying?' He said to them, 'Come and see.' They came and saw where he was staying, and they remained with him that day ...

Reflection

We meet *another* John in our reading today – John the Baptist. This John's actions – as well as his words – point others to Jesus. When Jesus notices two of John's followers now starting to follow him instead, he asks them, 'What are you looking for?' They can't really explain what they are looking for, they just know it's him. The disciples, like many in our world today, are looking for a light in the darkness. They are looking for meaning and truth.

Jesus responds with a simple invitation to them – and to all who are looking for something they can't quite explain – 'Come and see,' he says. Come with me, walk with me. Seek and you will find. With those three simple words, he offers an open invitation to discover life in all of its fullness.

INVITATION

Can we be people who point to Christ with our whole lives and in everything we do? Can we then invite others to come and see how gracious the Lord is?

Jesus Christ, Word made flesh, as we follow you day by day, may we invite others to come and see the abundant life you offer each of us. Amen.

AN INVITATION TO ... FIND REST

by Gemma Hunt

We've had three sleeps since celebrating Christmas Day. How has that sleep been for you?

Welcomed – after all the busyness of the preparations for the Big Day? Or still awaited – as you've still been non-stop visiting or entertaining? I'm definitely in the latter team, although I'd much prefer to be in the former!

This year I'm performing in a panto, which I love, it's a fun, festive show bringing joy to many, but it means it's been a busy season in a different way; entertaining a theatre full of audiences rather than a houseful for mince pies and pigs-in-blankets.

I'm sure, that, like you, I could do with a bit of a break soon. And I'm so grateful that Jesus offers each of us exactly that.

Read **Matthew 11:28-30**

At that time Jesus said, 'Come to me, all you that are weary and are carrying heavy burdens, and I will give you rest. Take my yoke upon you, and learn from me; for I am gentle and humble in heart, and you will find rest for your souls. For my yoke is easy, and my burden is light.'

Reflection

Today's reading can help us focus for a moment on who it is we are actually celebrating right now: Jesus. Jesus doesn't expect us to push ourselves beyond our capacity to celebrate his birthday with all the people we're seeing (or not seeing) at the moment. He simply invites us to 'come to me' for a good rest.

Whether we are feeling well-rested, still feeling a bit frantic, or even perhaps struggling to enjoy the festivities at all this year, I am certain that all of us could all do with putting our feet up and getting a good night's sleep. And remembering that Jesus didn't come to make us busy – but invites us to find rest.

INVITATION

Whatever is going on for you today – whether too much, too little or just about right – take time to hear Jesus' invitation and rest.

Loving Jesus, thank you for your invitation to all of us to take a break, which we gladly receive with humble gratitude. Amen.

AN INVITATION TO ... MAKE A JOYFUL NOISE

by Zeb Soanes

Working in radio at peculiar hours, I've had to be on duty for many a Christmas Day.

All too often, Christmas would suddenly arrive without the build-up and expectation of Advent which I loved as a child – and then it was over.

So, in busy December, I relish the opportunity to sing carols: at services, concerts or in the local square. Singing the nativity story together brings a grounding connection to Christmases and generations past, who have done just the same.

A moment's pause from thoughts of work or the busyness of the season to be thankful, cherish those we love and wonder at that first Christmas ...

Read Psalm 95.1-7

O come, let us sing to the Lord;
let us make a joyful noise to the rock of our salvation!
Let us come into his presence with thanksgiving;
let us make a joyful noise to him with songs of praise! ....
O come, let us worship and bow down,
let us kneel before the Lord, our Maker!
For he is our God, and we are the people of his pasture,
and the sheep of his hand.

Reflection

The theme of this year's reflections is 'The Great Invitation'. In today's psalm we are invited to come into the Lord's presence with thanksgiving.

There is always much to be thankful for. And by accepting invitations to make a joyful noise through the singing of hymns and carols we have a welcome opportunity to set aside the busyness of our own inner minds. To wonder at the ancient story. To feel connected with those who have marvelled long before us as we – 'the sheep of his hand' – mark the turning of the year, united in songs of praise.

INVITATION

I invite you to use music over the next few days to pause from the great bustle of Christmas, to reflect on all that you have to be thankful for and to feel the companionship of creation.

Lord, help us to find stillness to empty our minds of the everyday and to give thanks. Amen.

AN INVITATION TO ... **UNEXPECTED JOY**

by Matt Woodcock

Our twin girls were born over Christmas. I love sharing with them – despite their embarrassed protests – our laughter and struggle in welcoming them into the world.

It was my life's most unexpected joy moment. Just ahead of the time York City beat Man Utd 3-0 in the Cup. We were originally told that us having kids would be virtually impossible. Yet years later we found ourselves staring aghast at a hospital monitor. Seeing a heartbeat flash up on screen – and then another one. Months later we were changing nappies. (A somewhat less joyful experience.)

I've discovered that the journey of life and faith is always full of the unexpected. Navigating those times and moments often takes great trust and courage. And, for me, a faith to cling to.

… Sarah laughed to herself, saying, 'After I have grown old, and my husband is old, shall I have pleasure?' The Lord said to Abraham, 'Why did Sarah laugh, and say, "Shall I indeed bear a child, now that I am old?" Is anything too wonderful for the Lord? At the set time I will return to you, in due season, and Sarah shall have a son.'

Reflection

In today's reading, the elderly Sarah reacts to the seemingly impossible news of her impending motherhood with laughs of shocked disbelief It's the Bible's ultimate 'You can't be serious?!' moment. Yet her fleeting laughter soon turned to lasting joy when God's unexpected promise was beautifully fulfilled.

From Mary's angelic visitation to the twists-and-turns journey of the Wise Men, the Christmas story is full of surprises. A reminder that we follow a God who invites the most unlikely people to trust and follow him. To see hope and possibility when all seems lost.

It's on walking this narrow path of the often unexpected that we find our deepest joy in God. And, in my experience, plenty of laughter along the way.

INVITATION

Jesus invites us all to a life of unexpected joy and adventure. Where might he be calling you to trust him – however surprising or implausible it may seem?

Generous God of the unexpected, fill us with joy and laughter in abundance. Help us to trust your purposes for our lives. Amen.

AN INVITATION TO ... **OPEN THE DOOR**

by Bishop Rose Hudson-Wilkin

In 1983 I drove to the airport in Montego Bay. In a couple of weeks, I was to be married.

As I got closer to the airport, I realised that I was feeling anxious.

My fiancée was due in on a flight. Ken and I had met at college in England. I had returned to live and work in Jamaica, so we had been apart for a year.

On arrival at the airport, I was met by a friend who invited me through some doors for a better view of the disembarking passengers. Soon there he was. He looked very different! With not seeing him for a long time, I was able to connect with why I was anxious. Would he be as I remembered him? Would I still feel the same way about him? Or he about me?

14

Read **Revelation 3.7b; 20,21**

These are the words of the holy one, the true one... Listen! I am standing at the door, knocking; if you hear my voice and open the door, I will come in to you and eat with you, and you with me.

Reflection

The writer of Revelation draws our attention to the important role played by 'the door' in the great invitation. The door creates curiosity and an expectation of 'what is to come' or 'what lies behind or beyond the door!' Looking back, I am grateful that I accepted the invitation to go through the door and get a little closer. Accepting the invitation, allowed me to identify and own my anxieties. I am delighted to share that we have been happily married for over 39 years.

Our fears and anxieties can prevent us from taking the steps towards the door. Christ is at the door – let us open the door and welcome him into our lives. What a feast of opportunity awaits us as we follow the star this Christmas through the open door.

INVITATION

As a nation we have the opportunity to embrace change as we welcome our new Monarch, who himself has had to step through the door. This New Year's Eve, I invite you to pause from all the hustle and bustle and picture your own hopes and dreams for 2023. In the stillness, perhaps we can hear the door being knocked. Let's get ready to open it.

Dear God, thank you for being persistent in your knocking and for remaining at the door. May we find the courage to step outside our fears and open the door to your life of love. Amen.

AN INVITATION TO ... A FRESH START

by Ian Adams

Today, I'm dreaming of mountains.

Now I love where I live, but it's far from any mountains. So I need to dream big!

One of the things that kept me afloat during the pandemic was the hope that I might one day be in the mountains again. In their wild and magnificent company, I encounter both my smallness, and my belonging. I am restored, perhaps even changed a little for good, and emboldened to enter whatever new season of life is coming up.

Now of course, the mountains can be a challenging environment. And they are not everybody's happy place. But you will have your own place of transformation: somewhere you can breathe deep, see more clearly, accept some re-shaping, and make a fresh start.

Read **Micah 4.1-4**

In days to come the mountain of the Lord's house shall be established as the highest of the mountains, and shall be raised up above the hills. Peoples shall stream to it, and many nations shall come and say: 'Come, let us go up to the mountain of the Lord, to the house of the God of Jacob; that he may teach us his ways and that we may walk in his paths …'

Reflection

In our reading from the Jewish Scriptures, the prophet Micah urges his people to make a fresh start. Drawing on a rich theme from their collective history he uses the imagery of journeying to the mountain, representing the place of God's presence. Micah's hearers would have understood the link in their context to Jerusalem, and specifically to the Temple.

Micah foresees the healing and transformation that may come about by being prayerfully present to God in this place – a possibility that can encourage us even now.

Imagine! Nations no longer at war. Every person at peace, at home, in a flourishing earth. A fresh start for the world is, in God's grace, possible. It can and must begin in each of us.

I invite you to resolve this year to go prayerfully and hopefully to a place that will enable you to find the transformation you seek. To go into the mountains, whatever that might look like for you.

God of grace, mercy and peace, help me to find a place of transformation, where I can be present to you and make the fresh start into which you are calling me. Amen.

AN INVITATION TO ... SEE A GREAT LIGHT

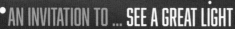

by Helen Dearnley

Where would you like to be this time next year?

I'm guessing your answer to that question isn't 'in prison'! However, that is where I hope still to be.

It is an incredible privilege to serve as a Prison Chaplain. Chaplains regularly see the potential for new beginnings for those in our care, and a hope that, though their pasts may have been in darkness, their futures can be so very different.

All of us have aspects of our past that I'm sure we would like to forget. I certainly do! However, simply forgetting the past will not allow for a different future. Understanding our past behaviours and learning from them allows us all an opportunity to change if we wish to.

'The people who sat in darkness have seen a great light ...' As Jesus walked by the Sea of Galilee, he saw two brothers, Simon, who is called Peter, and Andrew his brother, casting a net into the lake — for they were fishermen. And he said to them, 'Follow me, and I will make you fish for people.' Immediately they left their nets and followed him.

Reflection

To 'Follow the Star' this Christmas season we might need to step away from our past behaviours – just as the first disciples do in our reading. To be willing, like them, to take the actions we need to give ourselves the future we hope for.

Following Christ's call in this way is not necessarily about whole-life change - though it could be, if we follow a new career path, or invest more time in family and friends. But it can be much simpler, like choosing not to judge those who have made mistakes that have taken them to prison. Or finding it in our heart to forgive those who have grieved us personally.

To follow Christ is to find true freedom of heart and mind.

INVITATION

I invite you today to look at yourself in a new light, as the person you want to be – free from past mistakes and with a future full of the hope that following Christ brings.

God of hope and new beginnings, show us this day, we pray, the freedom that comes from following your example. Amen.

AN INVITATION TO ... EVERYONE

by Ben Woodfield

You receive a party invite. How do you respond?

It depends on the party, I hear you say.

My wife turned 40 this year and so we had a big party in our local pub. We wore '90s fancy dress, we laughed and we danced until the early hours. It was one of those social occasions where you look down at your watch and cannot believe where the time has gone. And what made it so special was the collection of people in the room – so many family and friends, many of whom hadn't seen each other for a long time.

Parties featured quite a lot in Jesus' life. He went to parties. He also spoke about parties in his teaching. And once or twice he did both at the same time ...

Read Luke 14.12-15

Jesus said also to the one who had invited him, 'When you give a banquet, invite the poor, the crippled, the lame, and the blind. And you will be blessed, because they cannot repay you, for you will be repaid at the resurrection of the righteous.'

Reflection

There's nothing quite like hearing about a party that you weren't invited to. I would suggest that's because in each of us there is a yearning to know: 'Am I welcome? Am I invited?'

Today's reading gives us an insight into the sort of parties Jesus championed. Jesus's parties involve unlikely people. Folks who may feel unwelcome, uninvited, and unable to return the favour.

The pub where we celebrated my wife's 40th is in the same place we meet for church every Sunday: a building at the heart of the Bolton council estate where we live. Our church services sometimes feel like the sort of parties Jesus talks about. None of us are there because we are important or popular. We are there because in God's kingdom there is a place for everyone. Jesus has invited us, and we have said 'yes'.

INVITATION

Jesus says to each of us today: 'You are invited, and you are welcome.' How will you respond to Jesus' invitation? How might accepting it transform your life – and the lives of those around you?

Jesus, help us to say yes to your invitation. And help us to welcome others to join the generous feast of your kingdom. Amen.

AN INVITATION TO ... **RUN THE RACE**

by Anne Wafula Strike

When I was a born in rural Kenya, my father felt sure I was destined to achieve great things so he gave me the second name 'Olympia' – after the home of the ancient Greek gods and of the famous sporting competition.

Though after I contracted polio at the age of two and was left paralysed from the waist downwards, no one imagined I would go on to win any races.

The years that followed included many struggles to take part in things many of my able-bodied peers took for granted – education, social life, romance, parenthood. During all these, my father would always encourage me to focus not on my problems but on my achievements: the obstacles I had – with encouragement and support from family, teachers and friends – already overcome.

Read **Hebrews 12.1-2**

Therefore, since we are surrounded by so great a cloud of witnesses, let us also lay aside every weight and the sin that clings so closely, let us run with perseverance the race that is set before us, looking to Jesus the pioneer and perfecter of our faith, who for the sake of the joy that was set before him endured the cross, disregarding its shame, and has taken his seat at the right hand of the throne of God.

Reflection

It's hard to persevere in the face of suffering and setbacks – but almost everyone who has achieved something great in life has faced struggle and obstacles along their way. Today's reading encourages us to remember that we are not alone in our struggles. Not only are we surrounded by a great cloud of witnesses – those who've gone before and travel alongside us – we also have the example of Jesus, who endured so much suffering along his path to glory.

After many setbacks and much heartache, eventually I did fulfil my father's Olympic dreams for me – competing in wheelchair racing at the Paralympics in Athens, and going on to win Bronze in the World Cup in Manchester. How did I make it to the finish line? Through trusting in God. With the support of my family. And by never giving up.

Whatever struggles or worries you may be facing as this New Year begins, why not spend some time remembering the struggles you have come through? And place your future in God's hands.

Jesus, be near anyone who feels they can't go on today.
Help us all to look to you for inspiration and hope
whatever lies ahead of us. Amen.

AN INVITATION TO ... TAKE ANOTHER ROAD

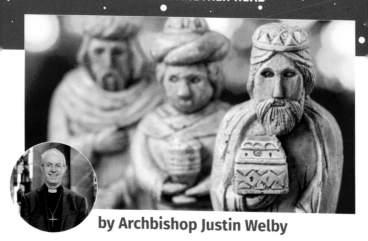

by Archbishop Justin Welby

Many years ago, I encountered a religious community called 'Chemin Neuf'. It's a Roman Catholic community, but people join from different Christian denominations, living together to witness to the God who calls each of us.

Chemin Neuf is French for 'new way'. I naturally assumed that this referred to the radical new way they had chosen to live together. No, I was told – New Way was actually the name of the road in Lyon, France, where the first Chemin Neuf Community was founded.

And yet they do represent a new way. It's a way of living in community across difference and disagreement. That's why, when I became Archbishop of Canterbury, I invited them to begin a new ecumenical community at Lambeth Palace: The Community of St Anselm.